MODERN FINE GLASS

AMERICAN

Cut crystal vase designed by John M. Gates for exhibit by Steuben at the Paris International Exposition of 1937

MODERN FINE *Glass*

LELOISE DAVIS SKELLEY

GARDEN CITY PUBLISHING CO., INC., GARDEN CITY, N. Y.

1942
GARDEN CITY PUBLISHING CO., INC.

SET UP BY BROWN BROTHERS LINOTYPERS
ENGRAVINGS MADE BY EAGLE PHOTO-ENGRAVING COMPANY
PRINTED IN THE UNITED STATES OF AMERICA
BY THE FERRIS PRINTING COMPANY

PREFACE

A DISPLAY of all the glass herein discussed would, indeed, be a sparkling, bewildering maze; in fact, even those well informed on glass might experience a little confusion and perplexity at the diminished grandeur of the finer wares in such levelling proximity. However remote the possibility of such a visual experience, with its mute challenge to the powers of description, there is always the question of individual taste and judgement. Not that the beauty of glass demands interpretation through criteria; its positive attributes unquestionably remove it from the province of esoteric beauty.

Nevertheless the rich diversity of thought and craftsmanship embodied in modern fine glass has raised it to such a lofty plane that some of its utter niceties often escape the casual observer. Even one versed in art in general misses a certain incremental beauty in glass if unfamiliar with some of its background. It is hoped that this brief volume will fill some background gaps for those interested in glass and be an introduction to representative modern fine glass of the world.

L. D. S.

CONTENTS

--◄{ CONTENTS }►--

Chapter VIII

ILLUSTRATIONS

Cut crystal vase, Gates-Steuben, Paris Exposition, 1937 . *Frontispiece*

VENETIAN

AUSTRIAN

CZECHOSLOVAKIAN

GERMAN

FRENCH

ILLUSTRATIONS

MODERN FINE GLASS

Chapter I

INTRODUCTION

VIRTUALLY every attribute of lovely glass is a residual product of centuries of toil and experimentation, slowly evolving through the heat of the furnace and the minds of men; and not infrequently major results were obtained as by-products of disappointment. For instance in 1670, when Johann Kunckel, the Silesian alchemist, produced his famous ruby glass by the addition of gold and tin, it came as a frustration of his hope of discovering, in glass, some sort of catalytic power for transmuting the tin to gold. Throughout the history of glass there have been many similar instances. Although this volume is devoted primarily to modern glass it seems logical to approach the subject through some of its interesting history.

Archaeological findings and some conservative conjecture unofficially date certain Egyptian glass pieces at 5000 B.C., but a less questionable date would be the late predynastic period, before 3400 B.C., as shown by findings of pale green glass beads in graves of that time. Fairly definite evidence indicates that glass was made in northern Mesopotamia about 2000 B.C. Free from any speculation, however, are the definite Egyptian records dating back to 1550 B.C., as, for instance, the blue glass bottle of Thothmes III in the

British Museum. Also small gem imitations, amulets, beads, and crystalline scarabs have been found, as well as large ewers, urns, unguent bottles, and vases of various colors, especially blues, yellows, greens, and some reds. At Tel-el-Amarna, Sir Flinders Petrie excavated several complete glass factories which apparently operated about 1370 B.C.

From the eighteenth dynasty, 1400 B.C., to the advent of the Christian era, Egyptian glass utensils were chiefly of three types: core wound, pad glass and tube blown glass (not to be confused with bubble blown glass). In making the thread or core-wound type, semi-fused threads or rods of glass were wound around a baked sand form, after which the surface was re-fused and finished and the sand removed. The second type, pad glass, was produced by spreading and rolling a mass of molten glass over a slab of marble. Utensils were then fashioned from these pads by rolling them into hollow shapes, on to which spouts, bases, handles, and lips were fused. Other simpler utensils were also made by pressing these semi-fused pads into hollow molds. The third type, which quite generally superseded pad glass, was tube blown glass. In this process a pad of semi-fused glass was wound around a metal tube; the tube of glass thus shaped was then closed, reheated and blown by the workman. It was only a step from this process to the bubble blowing procedure which has been used continuously since then. In this method the operator blows directly into a blob of molten glass on the end of the blowpipe. Some involved techniques were developed from these various methods, such, for instance, as the stratified rod glass and the stratified layer glass. Before the latter died out there were left specimens which, even today, stand out as marvellous among the world's best glass.

In Assyria during King Sargon's time, about 700 B.C., glass bottles were produced; and a blue glass termed Uknu, similar to lapis lazuli, is described on some cuneiform tablets, of about 650 B.C., excavated in Assyria. Later Alexandria, with natron from her adjacent lakes, became an active glass center, exporting her wares to all corners of the Roman Empire. Rome, Constantinople, and Venice followed Egypt in glassmaking; and from Venice the art gradually spread over Europe.

The Phoenicians, those renowned traders and merchants of antiquity, were also glassmakers of merit; they produced beads, bottles, vases, and other pieces, most of which were made of white glass. At Sidon, in the first century A.D., there appeared the unexcelled ivory paste glass, an opaque, non-reflecting ware, made in opaque white, emerald green, clay blue, and red. It has not been duplicated or equalled in beauty. Perhaps twenty centuries may endow some of our modern glass with an unfathomable beauty that will also defy duplication. As typical Phoenician glass has been excavated in almost every land where Phoenicians traded, it seems logical to conclude that they were among the first peoples to produce and utilize glass commercially. It was these Phoenicians whom Pliny the Elder cast as principals in his amusing account of the origin of glass. Whatever their part in the origin of glass, the Phoenicians are generally credited with the invention of glass blowing early in the Christian era. But there are indications that the blowpipe had been used far earlier in a limited way; in the Museum at Bologna there are specimens, from an earlier period, of peculiar beads which apparently were blown.

Evidently glass and its possibilities did not appeal to the Greeks as did the other fine arts, for there is a surprising scarcity of glass articles compared with their superb artistic creations in other lines.

The Romans, however, became leaders in glass work and far surpassed most of their neighbors who were older at the craft. Of all their charming work the cameo glass unquestionably excelled in its beauty and craftsmanship; inspired perhaps by the beauty of the semi-precious natural onyx stone, with its orderly translucent and opaque strata. Examples of this Roman method of working and cutting glass cameo fashion are: the exquisite Moore vase in America, the Naples vase, Auldjo oil pitcher, and the Portland vase in the British Museum. In 1848 the physical make-up of the Portland vase was revealed, when a crazed sailor visiting the British Museum smashed the vase. It appeared to be a molded pad glass composed of three parts. Found in the sarcophagus, supposedly, of Septimius Servius, it is generally regarded as Graeco-Roman of early imperial date, between 50 B.C. and A.D. 50.

Following their mastery of other glassworking procedures, the Romans were among the first to sense the fuller possibilities of blown glass. Before the end of the third century A.D. it was in general domestic use, and, even beyond table needs, they made glass for various household and personal uses, such as jewel containers, dice, and ornaments. Their exceptional ability as glassmakers is lucidly illustrated in the story of the young Emperor Heliogabalus (A.D. 205–222), a mixture of Roman gourmet and practical joker. He seated a houseful of guests at a table loaded to overflowing with tempting foods, fruits, nuts, and elaborate decorations; everything on the table was made of glass!

As Rome approached its decline, glass attained a barbaric splendor, amazing in its garish achievements. Gross disproportions appeared, disguised in unexcelled techniques such as the diatreta cutting, and other masterly processes. Weird and fantastic things were necessary to satisfy the jaded populace, who had thrown off all restraint as they sped to dissolution. Numerous examples of this garish glass have been found in German, French, and Italian tombs.

When Byzantine glassmakers came into prominence in the fourth and fifth centuries, their wares for a time were quite Roman in decoration—an expected trend in the wake of Constantine and his wide Romanization of Byzantium. They followed cameo cutting and other Roman methods in their work, but later veered to the use of enamels, gilts, and plain glass bold relief, accomplished by cutting with a disc. The twelve Hedwig tumblers are of this high glass relief Byzantine style, but lately have been ascribed to the work of Egyptians. The much chronicled Holy Grail supposedly was started on its nomadic existence by a Byzantine glass maker.

From the fifth to the fifteenth century the glass industry disintegrated just as did European civilization in general. Many methods were forgotten or largely obliterated, and hollow glassware narrowed down to poorly made jug-like beakers, just a step ahead of baked clay. As far as the glass industry was concerned during these bleak years, the dead actually functioned more advantageously than the living; the entombed spirits of many illustrious men of better days were standing vigilant guard over such masterpieces as the Portland vase and others, preserving them for more appreciative ages.

The next revival came through the Arabs and Syrians who produced some remarkable glass between the ninth and fourteenth centuries. Examples of their work reached Europe through the Moors in Spain, and through pieces carried back by the early Crusaders. Among these were specimens of colored enamels, gold enamelling, lapis lazuli, and other mineral colored glass. The Venetians were paralleling some of this work from the sixth century on, but produced little glass of merit before the Renaissance.

This brief historical sketch of glass and glassmaking clearly places glass among man's early manufacturing endeavors. Although the records give fairly accurate dates to some of the early glass pieces, these are unquestionably antedated many centuries by undated findings. Speculation might easily picture a piece of hollowed crystalline quartz in use during the Stone Age, in which event true crystal may have seen prehistoric service.

Without the aid of conjecture, however, it is safe to say that glassmaking has had a continuous history almost from the beginning of our recorded history, and that glassmaking has always been considered a venerable art and held in highest esteem. "The glass industry was the only one in which noblemen, to whom all manual labor meant degradation, could give themselves up without lowering themselves: glass-workers were gentlemen" (Edmond Haraucourt in *Medieval Manners Illustrated* at the Cluny Museum). "In Italy and France the craft was so greatly esteemed that a nobleman might marry into the family of a gentilhomme verrier without dishonor" (Whitefriars).

Glassmaking, that long and highly complicated procedure of transforming a blob of molten substance into objects of beauty, is exceedingly interesting and instructive to those unacquainted with the glass industry. Glass in general is shaped by blowing, pressing, and casting. These three methods involve the use of molten glass which necessitates subsequent gradual cooling, to insure uniform contraction throughout the body of the glass. This gradual cooling process, termed annealing, minimizes porosity and imparts strength and durability to the glass.

Glassware is made of silicic acid and an alkali compounded with other ingredients, chiefly lead, lime, potash, calcium, nitrate, alumina (which reduces fusibility) and many metallic oxides for coloring. These materials vary with the type of glass desired. Addition of decolorizing agents, such as manganese and arsenic, neutralizes the impurities found in sand, particularly iron particles. Lead and lime are of such importance in determining the quality of the glass, that the final product is usually classified either as lead or lime glass, depending on the ingredient used. The lead product has a brilliant finish, is heavy, has a resonant ring, and is the foundation of most genuine cut glass. Extremely tough and elastic in the molten state it is readily blown into delicate shapes. "The use of lead in glassmaking was not precisely a modern discovery. Clear glass of the Roman period has occasionally been met with, and ancient opaque red glass contains lead. The glass of the Middle Ages called 'Jewish Glass,' also had lead in its composition; but these do not seem to have contained potash (usually pearl ash imported from Canada or Russia), as did the English flint" (Editorial Staff, *Mentor Magazine*, April 15, 1919).

Lime glass lacks the brilliant luster, has a less resonant ring, and is of lighter weight than lead glass, but its ductility, lighter weight and lower cost make it the ideal base for most commercial pressed glass. A rare exception is the utilization of a lime base for the exquisite Venetian glass in which ductility is a prime requisite for the execution of their intricate designs and gossamer decorations; cutting and engraving are rather uncommon to Venetian decoration.

Table and decorative glass ordinarily carry some decoration which, for simplicity and understanding, may be classified into two groups. First are the types of decoration imparted to the glass in the semi-fused and molten stages; that is, by molds such as those used in pressed glass, molded glass, and cast glass. There is also the type of mold into which much fine glass is blown to impart the exterior shape; in this process the operator's breath inflates the semi-fused glass against the walls of the mold. Most blown tumblers are made in this way. In this first group other decorative features in the shapes are derived from free blowing, swinging, and cutting of the semi-fused glass, and from coloring by metallic oxides, and other means, in the molten state. The second group comprises all other types of decoration; that is, cutting the surface by hand or machine or by chemicals, and decoration by application of some substance to the glass such as metal, enamel, paint, another layer of glass, or even threads and bands of glass, as in much of the Venetian.

Chapter II

ITALY AND SPAIN

ITALIAN, CRISTALLO, MURANO, VENETIAN

ONE of the earliest dated records of Venetian glass is that of a shipment of glass mosaics A.D. 580 to the island of Grado where the cathedral Santa Eufemia was being rebuilt. The Venerable Bede later recorded that a Venetian glass window was ordered about the year 652 for Benedict Biscop's great church and monastery at Wearmouth, England. Not before the Renaissance, however, did the glass commonly known as Venetian reach any degree of perfection. In 1291, due to severe labor regulations and fire hazard in Venice, the glass-ovens were moved to the island of Murano, which has remained to this day the center of Venetian glasscraft. These early Murano craftsmen, artists rather than glassworkers, produced marvels which rivalled and surpassed much earlier glass. They used many and varied shapes, colored with the famous girasole (opal), aquamarina, rubino, lattimo, giallo d'oro, and others, making the Murano workmen the envy of all the world during the sixteenth century. This early Venetian glass has been classified into ten groups, many of which are still produced at Murano: (1) vessels of colored glass; (2) gilt and enamelled glass; (3) crackled glass; (4) latti-

Nineteenth Century Vase

(Courtesy of Metropolitan
Museum of Art)

Modern vase and natural color glass lemon

A modern creation in which two hands carry a rose colored opaque bowl, sprinkled with gold

(Courtesy of S. A. Venini, Murano)

cinio, lattimo, or lattisuol; (5) lace or filigree glass; (6) mil-
lefiori (thousand flowers); (7) variegated, or marble
opaque; (8) splashed glass; (9) painted glass; and (10)
engraved glass.

It is reasonable to conclude that the Venetians took a
questionable course in attempting to meet Bohemian competition in the eighteenth century with a non-typical Venetian product. Had they not virtually turned their backs on
their own accepted styles and designs in attempting to produce a heavier cut ware to meet this new competition,
Venetian glass might have escaped its century of waning
popularity. Dr. Antonio Salviatti evidently followed a similar line of reasoning in 1856 when he partially revived the
industry by returning to typical designs but of less elaborate
ornamentation.

Modern Venetian glass has borrowed many of its quaint,
intriguing little decorative frills from the old Murano cristallo, whose dainty prancing sea-horses, dolphins, and
winged dragons welcome this new opportunity to vie for
favor in another century, though their capers are somewhat
restrained.

Probably the chief claim of Venetian glass to recognition
among the world's many glasses is individuality. Hand
blowing and decorating carry into the ware characteristic
minor irregularities which are not unwelcome or unsightly,
but rather delightfully refreshing amidst our modern excess
of perfection. Unobjectionable tiny flaws, such as occasional minute bubbles, unevenness in gold dusting, or per-

VENETIAN

Jar, figurines and fruits in crystal; filigree work and decoration in purple black. Product of Venini, Murano

(Courtesy of S. A. Venini, Murano)

[PAGE 29]

haps a slight "Pisa effect" in vase or bottle neck do not detract from Venetian glass. Although such imperfections are not sought by the creator of the glass or by the purchaser, they will probably continue to appear until some wandering Robot lands on Murano Island.

Although the extremely ornate Venetian pieces, flanked with denizens of the deep, shells and swags, flowers, flutings, and furbelows innumerable, compose an inviting background for color they suggest little restraint. This accounts, in part, for the amazing use of colors in the Venetian glass, which run the chromatic scale from crystal to black, employing the daintiest delicate shades in some pieces, while bold, clashing colors produce kaleidoscopic effects in others.

The many designs, shapes, and colors in Venetian glass offer a wide range for selection to match almost any dining room ensemble. Especially does it complement the dainty Belleeks and other thin chinas, and it nicely offsets earthenware such as Italian Majolica in which it intensifies the national motif and adds a note of lightness. Water glasses, goblets, and other pieces which are handled by the diner are surprisingly light and truly a joy to behold.

In the realm of table decoration Venetian glass is most entrancing, with its interesting and colorful designs in centerpieces, candlesticks, and candelabra. Other ornamental pieces, such as the finial, transform candle holders into pedestals for quaint little figures which do daylight duty when candles are not needed.

VENETIAN

Vase, bowl and opaque glass fruit by Venini

(Courtesy of S. A. Venini, Murano)

[PAGE 31]

Some general distinguishing features of Venetian glass are: the uneven, rough pontil mark; extremely light weight; occasional bubbles; characteristic maritime decorations; quite often slight irregularities in shape and symmetry; and alluring designs and shapes, some of which are actually bewitching in their whimsey and gay unrestraint.

SPAIN

Roman domination brought to Spain Roman glass factories, which continued under various incoming peoples and influences long after Rome had withdrawn her proconsuls. After the eleventh century the Moorish Oriental influence crept in, especially around Almeria and the other southern glass centers. Catalonia and Barcelona followed more the Venetian trends. Naturally a compromise product followed in the sixteenth century in the enamelled ware which was typically "Venetian" in shapes but noticeably "East" in spirit of decoration. Cut, gilt, luster, and printed glasses were produced from early eighteenth century on, especially at Villanueva di Alcorcon and La Granja de San Ildefonso.

The glass of José Gol of Barcelona is the only outstanding modern Spanish glass. His free use of translucent enamels of deep rich colors produces a distinctive glass despite a certain coarse heaviness and the incongruous Venetian touch on some pieces.

VENETIAN

Vases of black and crystal with milk white filigree by Venini

(*Courtesy of S. A. Venini, Murano*)

[PAGE 33]

Chapter III

AUSTRIA, CZECHOSLOVAKIA AND GERMANY

AUSTRIA

BOHEMIAN glass has regained its prestige among the world's fine glass, though the name is now more generic than national. Working with Viennese artists, Ludwig Lobmeyr (1829-1902) from 1870 on produced some excellent shapes and designs in cut and engraved glass; thus began the significant development of an un-Venetian type, though noticeable Italian Renaissance lines persisted in the shapes. Early in the twentieth century Lobmeyr introduced deep sunk decorative motifs on amazingly clear glass; a few skillfully plotted slashes accentuated this purity and transparency without resorting to prismatic effects. "Lobmeyr produces cut or engraved vases so skillfully formed that they remind us of the lovely natural crystals of the Renaissance lapidaries."

J. & L. Lobmeyr, working with many prominent artists, more recently have recaptured in a modern way the best of old Bohemia's spirit and design in their exquisitely engraved vases, bowls, urns and innumerable other creations. Among their illustrious artistic collaborators in cut and engraved

AUSTRIAN

Table set in white cut crystal; chandelier with a black cut glass base and pendeloques for four candles,
designed by E. J. Wimmer, Vienna

(Courtesy of J. and L. Lobmeyr, Vienna)

[PAGE 35]

crystal work, Lobmeyr include: Michael Powolny, Jaroslav Horejc, Ena Rottenberg, Marianne Rath, Rudolf Rothemund, J. E. Wimmer, and formerly Kolo Moser. In their modern adaptations of Muslin glass as revived by Stefan Rath and Oswald Haerdtl, Lobmeyr have produced a lighter, more lustrous glass of newer designs and shapes, sometimes even tinted; and despite such striking variations, they have retained the old Muslin glass character. Among Lobmeyr favorites are the cameo cut crystal, modern Muslin, and the striking black enamel with its designs varying from simple foliage to human figurines.

Other ideas in Austrian glass have been borrowed from the creations of the Wiener Werkstätte in Vienna, where J. Hoffmann, M. Powolny, and other glass wizards have applied their genius to the production of beautiful and usable glass. Especially have they striven for and achieved pleasing lines and shapes in the work-a-day pieces such as water sets, dessert glasses, and heavy crystal covered bowls. Some authorities label the products of the Wiener Werkstätte as laborious and too academic; however, such opinions are perhaps a bit hypercritical.

At Stockerau, Austria, the distinctive impress and inspiration of Kolo Moser reappeared in the striking copper ruby cut glass of L. Forstner who has also done new things in Ueberfang style (two layers of different color glass, blown one inside the other).

The Bimini Werkstätte in Vienna, aside from the produc-

AUSTRIAN

Crystal vase "Diana" in intaglio engraving, designed by Ena Rottenberg for Lobmeyr

(Courtesy of J. and L. Lobmeyr, Vienna)

[PAGE 37]

AUSTRIAN
Heavy cut and engraved crystal wine set by Lobmeyr
(Courtesy of J. and L. Lobmeyr, Vienna)
[PAGE 38]

AUSTRIAN
Candlesticks and fruit bowl in Muslin glass by Lobmeyr
(Courtesy of J. and L. Lobmeyr, Vienna)
[PAGE 39]

tion of playful, airy figurines, creates an astonishingly thin and filmy tableware not unlike Muslin glass, and other net patterns strikingly reminiscent of Venetian latticini. This thin glass work has achieved much of its individuality through the work of the Bimini artists, Fritz Lampl and Artur Berger; the white thread glass of the latter is an exceedingly brilliant design.

CZECHOSLOVAKIA

Although Czechoslovakian glass has developed along lines quite parallel to those of Austria and Germany, its glass is distinctive in ornamentation and design, largely due to the influence of the artists directing the state and city industrial schools.

Chief among them is Josef Drahonovsky at the Prague School of Industrial Art, whose inspiration and teaching have projected his influence into many Czechoslovakian factories. While still in his teens, Drahonovsky was engraving precious and semi-precious stones at the Turnov School; then he furthered his engraving studies in Vienna before taking up sculptural work at Prague.

From the fullness of this training and background Drahonovsky brings to glass every trait necessary to decorative cutting, including an uncanny awareness of nature and what it can lend to glass decoration. From massive ornamental cups to tiny crystal gems his work reflects his many-sided training. Strength of line, balance and other essentials of artistic composition are obvious in Drahonovsky's designs

CZECHOSLOVAKIAN

Ornamental glass engraved after design by Josef Drahonovsky, Prague School of Industrial Art

(Courtesy of Professor Drahonovsky)

CZECHOSLOVAKIAN

Upper, blown figurines by A. Brychta of the Zelezny-Brod State School; lower, bowls by K. Moser

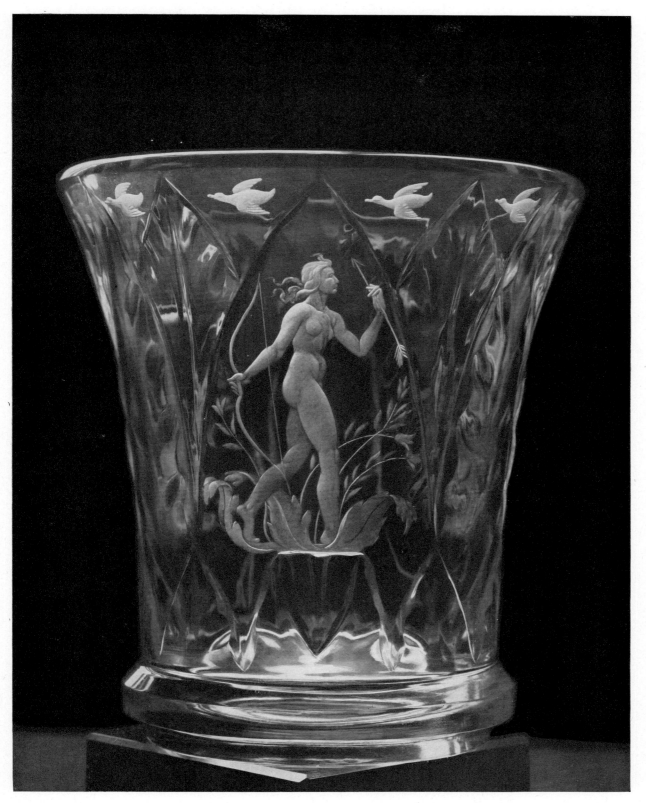

CZECHOSLOVAKIAN

Intaglio engraved "Diana" vase by Josef Drahonovsky of the Prague School of Industrial Art

(Courtesy of Professor Drahonovsky)

〔PAGE 43〕

only as elements of a unifying grace; never do they compete within the unit they support. Unquestionably Drahonovsky's glass must be ranked with the world's best.

At the State School in Bor-Haida, Czechoslovakia, where Josef Gerner associated with R. Cizek, J. Scrotter, Professor Pfohl, J. Oertel, and others are directing the course of things glass, the designs and decorations are characterized by disc engraving surrounded by free clear cutting.

At the Steinschonau School, Eiselt and E. Kroner are doing engaging things in feathery engraved decorations and enamels. At Zelezny-Brod, Juna, Zak and Prenosyl the older traditions are followed in Bohemian engraving, while A. Metelak and A. Brychta are adding some artistic figurines and Venetian type things. The typically Czechoslovakian products of J. Horejc are usually among Lobmeyr's most attractive glass in Vienna. Other noteworthy Czechoslovakian glass is originating in the Lotz and Moser factories; especially in the latter, the present location of C. LeBeau who formerly did so much for Dutch glass at Leerdam.

BOHEMIAN GLASS

Before the fifteenth century, Bohemian glass could hardly claim a nationality of its own, inasmuch as it was so similar to Bavarian glass, an early German potash glass, which likewise originated in the Bohemian forests. The ideas and efforts of three men gave early Bohemian glass the impetus which ultimately pushed Venetian glass off Europe's finest tables and made Bohemian the dominating

CZECHOSLOVAKIAN

Upper, glass from Prague Industrial School; left, vases by
A. Metelak; right, vase by J. Horejc

[PAGE 45]

glass until the whims and caprices of fashion turned to the sparkling English and Irish flint glass.

These three men so important in Bohemian glass history were: first, that art loving, queer recluse, Holy Roman Emperor Rudolph II (1552-1612), who imported Milan rock crystal engravers to Prague and successfully made a heavy glass in imitation of rock crystal (genuine rock crystal is cut directly from white crystalline quartz); second, Caspar Lehmann, the German engraver, brought to Prague by Rudolph in 1590, who cut, engraved, and decorated this new Bohemian ware in true rock crystal style; third, Johann Kunckel, the Silesian alchemist who in 1670 first put color into the new Bohemian glass. His famous ruby glass was produced by the addition of gold and tin to the molten glass. Judging from present prices of this old ruby glass, Kunckel's alchemy included a bit of economics.

By the end of the seventeenth century, Bohemian glass had acquired a definite individuality characterized by massive crystal glass of rugged shapes, colored or uncolored, and decorated with most positive engraving. With the addition of calcium to the forest potash base, the Bohemian glass achieved a crystal clarity previously unknown. Deep cut engraving methods carried over from rock crystal work, found ideal background and ample metal for bold intaglio decorations and for lighter engraving and etching. They particularly favored the heavy intaglio engraving which imparted unusual perspective and realism to their imperial eagles and electors, escutcheons, and other decorative

BOHEMIAN

Upper right, old Bohemian standing cup decorated with engraved hunting scene, 1710; lower left, eighteenth century Bohemian standing cup, decorated in gold foil and colors between two layers of glass

(Cups, Courtesy of Metropolitan Museum of Art)

GERMAN

Center, modern engraved plate by Wilhelm von Eiff, Stuttgart School of Arts and Crafts

[PAGE 47]

devices. Etching and engraving were reserved for the lighter surface decorations, especially landscapes, portraits, coats-of-arms, emblems, and human figures, and the oft-recurring stag in the forest seen on the numerous decanters, toilet bottles and pitchers.

The first quarter of the eighteenth century saw Bohemian glass pass Venetian in popular favor, which position it maintained for some fifty years, when it surrendered to the English and Irish flint glass. Instead of meeting this new glass with a better Bohemian glass, Bohemian makers apparently got panicky and attempted new and strange designs—very much as did the Venetians when Bohemian glass appeared. In 1730 the Bohemians worked out something new, the "inserted gold" process in which they encased thin gold between the layers of double-walled goblets. More experiments and commercial modifications of this process might have proved less fatal to their prowess than the rococo products to which they turned. Though it never regained its dominating earlier position, Bohemian glass continued one of the recognized fine wares, and later its influence was evident in all glass of the Germanic and Low Countries. Today Bohemian glass is characterized by its remarkable clearness and deep and sharp cutting; qualities which have persisted through all Bohemian modifications and improvements.

GERMANY

Along the Rhine in Western Germany, as early as the third century, glass of considerable artistic merit was being made; ancient glass factories probably built by the Romans have been excavated at Worms, Trier (formerly Treves), Cologne and in the Eifel mountains. Old Rhenish graves have preserved and disclosed a number of gilt decorated bowls and beakers of the fondi d'oro type; a process in which inscriptions, figures, and scenes were etched out of a layer of gold, and subsequently covered with a film of transparent glass. From the third to the fifth century, this type of glass and ornament continued, with the pictured legends gradually assuming more of biblical and religious tenor. And during these same years there came into being that unmistakable label of German glass, the prunt— a quaint little knob or boss which has persisted to the present.

With general world decadence under way in the fifth century, the German glass industry lay virtually dormant until the late medieval years, though it did stir occasionally with the appearance of bits of crude work.

First to reawaken before 1400 was the Hessian country where the hills and woods soon became spotted with crude glass furnaces, all of which were producing the green beakers of characteristic cabbage stalk appearance; relieved only by rough prunts, spirals, or bosses, not unlike some of the bossed beakers unearthed at Pompeii.

In 1548 the tall, cylindrical, enamelled welcome-glasses (*humpen-willkomm* glasses) appeared from German furnaces, having previously been imported from Venice. Coincidentally the quaint old cabbage stalk beaker was evolving

GERMAN

Engraved crystal cup by Wilhelm von Eiff, Stuttgart School of Arts and Crafts

[PAGE 50]

into the roemer wine glass, whose grace and utility apparently have given it everlasting popularity.

Following this, opaque enamel on hollow glass, a Venetian process, found a great reception in Germany. It was the decorative vogue well into the seventeenth century. At Nurnberg and Munich, frank and wholesale emulation of Venetian glass was attempted; even imported Venetian workmen, however, could not obtain the light, airy figures from the potash glass; so the production turned to German lines. Incidentally these two towns, Nurnberg and Munich, claimed the first famous German glass cutter, George Schwanhardt who was born in the latter city and worked at Nurnberg. Three men were chiefly responsible for the ascendancy attained by Germany and Bohemia in the glass markets of the world in the early eighteenth century. They were (1) Emperor Rudolph II; (2) Caspar Lehmann, and (3) Johann Kunckel, whose works were discussed under Bohemian glass.

After being supplanted largely by the English and Irish flint glass during the latter part of the eighteenth century, German glass opened the nineteenth century with new decorations and designs which gave it about fifty years of fairly good business. In their new bid for popularity Mohn revived Schaper's translucent enamel painting; others tinted glass in the "metal" and some did striking imitations of Venetian ware, semi-precious stones, et cetera. Despite this display of technique, however, public whims and fancy soon veered from so much second-hand art and a decline set in.

Productions of the Zwiesel State School

[PAGE 52]

About 1860 when Lobmeyr started rebuilding the Austrian glass industry, Germany fell in with his plan and established several state schools for art similar to those of Austria and Czechoslovakia. Professor Bruon Mauder's influence at the school in Zwiesel has been responsible for some of Germany's best achievements in the field of glass. Painted vases, jars engraved after the fashion of "Biedermeyer" and beautifully ground and engraved goblets are among the products.

"The shapes are marked throughout by a simple grandeur and the decoration is developed directly out of the shape and out of the nature of the material. The finishing of the glass is so carried out that it closely follows the design and by a fine working of the surface it enhances the entire effect. In the engraved glass it is principally the delicacy and transparency of the material which are stressed, while with the painted glass richer effects are obtained which lend to the articles at times a most charming fantastic character." (Albert Dresdner, *Creative Art*, Jan. 1930.) Hans Mauder, the director's son, has done some excellent figure decoration.

The Deutsche Werkstätte in Munich has produced, with the artist Seyfried, some classic engraved glass adorned with his characteristic sport figures, small animal grotesques, et cetera. Especially attractive are his dessert pieces and drinking glasses. Other Munich artists working with the institute are Emmerich, Süsz, Rehm, Vietor, Hillerbrand, and Neeb-Seyfried.

Wilhelm von Eiff, of the Arts and Crafts School at Stuttgart, a painter as well as glass artist, is master of all types of glass cutting, from bold reliefs in his magnificent cameo work to the laciest intaglios. His artistry is applied also to quartz, rock crystal, lapis lazuli, onyx, and other semi-precious stones. The quality of von Eiff's work can be gauged by the fact that, prior to the war, he was making numerous objets d'art for René Lalique and his discriminating clientele.

Richard Süssmuth at Penzig in Silesia is outstanding in the realm of glass. His art seems built around a philosophy that there are no limitations imposed on the artist who expresses himself in glass. His figurative design mysteriously subordinates the glass to its effect, never assuming the appearance of an addenda. Geometric configurations always reveal a common origin with the shape of the piece. Prismatic calculations subtly guide some of his most "careless" slashes; and enhancing light refractions creep into designs to produce eerie nuances in the crystal.

The influence of Haertl and Benna at the Breslau trade school is felt throughout the Silesian factories and showrooms. Another German artist, Rudolph Ville, specializes in the application of true artistry to household glass; Walter Nitschke is recognized for his employment of delicate decorative lines of almost microscopic proportions; Karl Friedrich for his excellent colored glass; H. Sattler for his superb cut goblets. Among others who have done noteworthy work are Ida Paulin, Jean Beck, B. Bayerle and K. Bertsch.

Chapter IV

FRANCE

ALTHOUGH ancient glass factories have been excavated at Poitou, Lyons, Marne, and Vendee in France, and there is evidence of some glassmaking in the twelfth century, the trail is quite dim until somewhat later. "In the thirteenth century glass-working became general in France, and in the fourteenth century it already constituted a regular industry; the use of glass for table utensils was common enough in St. Louis's time to allow drinking-vases to be known under the name of 'glasses' no matter of what they were made." (From *Medieval Manners*, Cluny Museum, by Edmond Haraucourt). In the fifteenth century Venice and Altare glassworkers were welcomed into French factories where they were at home in imitating the Italian gilt and enamelled ware and other Venetian favorites.

The sixteenth century produced little French glass of artistic merit other than some enamelled ware and figurines from the Nevers works. The year 1665 witnessed the founding of the St. Gobian works.

Eighteenth century France was absorbed more with her industrial flat glass than with tableware and decorative glass, but with the general nineteenth century glass revival, T. J.

Broccard led the way for France with his Mohammedan glass and other imitations; especially enamelled and colored glass, and the sixteenth century German goblets. Following him were the three artists: E. Rousseau, Gallé, and Léveillé. Rousseau (1827-1891) was noted for his use of opaque ornaments on transparent colored glass; the significance of Léveillé centered around his furtherance of the traditions and ideas of Rousseau; and the great master Emile Gallé (1846-1904) will always be remembered for his ceaseless experimentation and adaptation of art principles to glass. These artists made France conscious of fine glass and its possibilities. Gallé's first accomplishment was transparent colored glass; then some individualistic engraving; in 1897 acid etching on laminated, multicolored opaque glass; and then much experimentation with pâte de verre (paste glass). Though his designs and shapes at times were excellent, Gallé's real contributions were in the fields of materials and ingredients.

The plastic glass process which lay hidden for centuries was rediscovered by Henri Cros about 1901. After much experimenting he achieved success by firing powdered cullett (bits of broken glass) in a refractory mold of fireclay which resulted in complete fusion. Although some table glass and other small pieces were produced, his lasting work with paste glass was the great decorative bas reliefs and other more or less sculptural works.

The next great step in plastic glass was made about 1920 by François Décorchemont, who produced the first hard, translucent plastic glass. His translucent, richly colored vases, bowls and the like have alluring velvety surfaces and depth of colorings seldom found in blown glass.

Often the work of Albert Dammouse is termed pâte de verre, but for the most part it is actually an enamel paste. Confusion arises from the fact that he almost achieved transparency in his very diaphanous porcelain. However, Dammouse's work usually is considered glass and as such is unique and captivating. M. Walters of Nancy is also an exponent of plastic glass.

Inherent limitations of this plastic glass, however, thwarted any chance of its supplanting blown glass, either as a working medium for artists or as a finished product, as far as tableware or decorative glass were concerned. M. Marinot, the next French artist of importance, worked with blown glass, following and improving upon the procedures of Rousseau, Léveillé, and Gallé. Marinot was designer, maker, and decorator of most of his best pieces. Handling the blowpipe personally, often in the very door of his furnace, he produced new and lovely things in glass. Prior to 1912, when he dropped painting for glass, his interests centered around colors; vivid opaques or clear glass with usually some decorative flowers, birds, or feminine heads. Then he turned to very thick walled glass, which opened up new possibilities in decoration. He cut and etched unusually bold relief designs and often incorporated secondary spreading color pigments within the body of the glass; and his use of bubbles in controlled designs was indeed a novelty.

FRENCH

Vase in semi-opaque opalescent glass by René Lalique

(Courtesy of Ovington's)

[PAGE 58]

FRENCH

Molded glass vase with parakeet design by Lalique

(Courtesy of Ovington's)

[PAGE 59]

René Lalique was represented at the Paris exhibition of 1900 and acclaimed, but in the field of jewelry rather than glass. Finding this field too limited for his ambitions and enamoured with crystal and glass, he started, about 1902, the manufacture of art pieces in the little bulb plant which he took over at Combs-la-Ville, in the suburbs of Paris. Soon he was creating worthwhile glass and gained quick recognition.

While Lalique was thus engaged, Gallé was acclaimed for productions in which he used superimposed layers of colored glasses to obtain effects similar to those of cameo engraving.

Lalique's approach to glass, however, was different. While Gallé was primarily a painter, Lalique is primarily a sculptor. He works through the crystalline purity of glass, always depending upon the sheer solidity of the pure hard glass for decorative foundation. Occasionally eerie tints embody in his glass ethereal shadows quite indescribable if one has not witnessed fairies capering under a fading rainbow. He is the rare combination of artist and practical man. With all his delicate shades, balance, and pleasing lines, the utility of the piece is his first consideration. Thus he subtly commands respect as well as admiration for the beautiful. This unusual artistic equilibrium, linked with technical knowledge and captivating decorative ideas, endows Lalique's creations with a natural individuality. The glass of some of his productions, in its peculiar iridescence, seems alive with phantom glows like that of the tomb-sea-

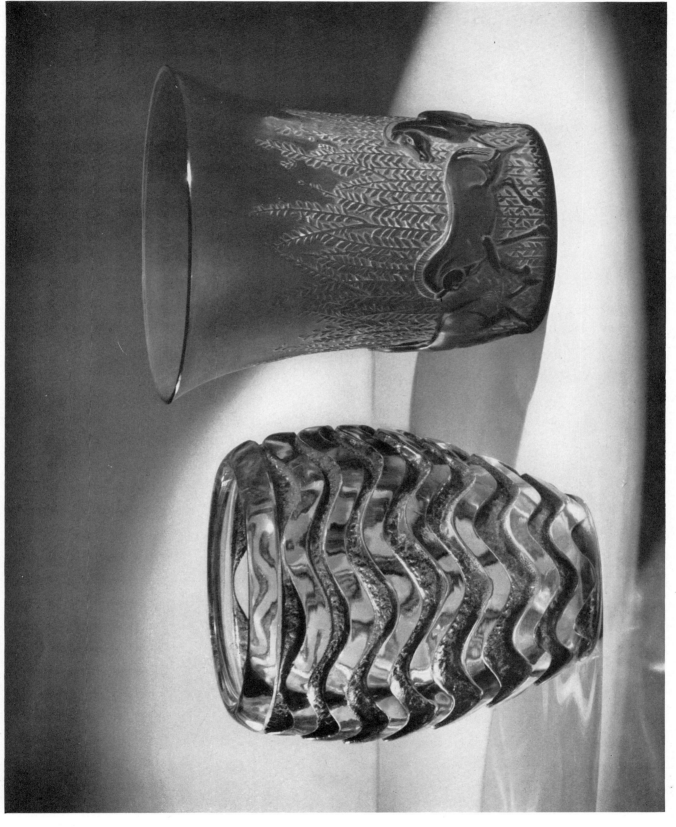

FRENCH

Lalique; left, vase in heavy acid etched style, semi-opaque; right, vase of molded glass with moving pony and reed design

(Courtesy of Ovington's)

[PAGE 61]

soned glass of the ancients. "For decorative effects he gets his inspirations from nature, adapting, however, the motif, with rare sagacity, to the object whose beauty it is to enhance."

His use of the cire perdue process (glass blown into clay molds) has enabled him to create unique pieces which have found their way into the homes of collectors of rare and unusual examples of artistic creation. Every design that comes out of his work-shop is Lalique's personal creation. The name LALIQUE is etched into each piece.

The Daum Brothers Glass Works at Nancy go back to 1875 when Auguste and Antonin Daum, sometime students of Gallé, started their glass experimentation. Their earliest efforts were with gold ornamentation, then Arabian glass decorated with scrolls and gold leaves. Following their "Egyptian" glass near the end of the nineteenth century they produced a colored glass by the "flushed" process, which has always been a Daum favorite. Almost from the beginning the brothers Daum have done acid etching and today they characterize most of their heavy pieces with the deep indentations of heavy engraving of the Gallé type; and naturally they have been influenced by the remarkable acid work of Marinot.

Henri Navarre's work also has been with heavy glass of massive shapes. He gets an unusual X-ray effect by uneven blotches of color in the inner glass. His work is not dissimilar to that of Marinot, but perhaps less individual.

The exquisite enamelled glass of Marcel Goupy has given him high rank among French artists. In his decorative designs the composition is always impelling in its balance though his work never reflects any pedantic slavery to art precepts. The vitrifiable color glaze, which he perfected in 1925, imparts an interesting marbling and iridescence to the glass.

Jean Luce, modernist, largely foregoes the use of figures and relief in his decorations, relying almost wholly on geometric designs and impersonal motifs for effects. Originally his glass decorations were for the most part enamels, but gradually he has added other processes. Many of his modern designs are executed by means of the sand blast which is quite adapted to regular curves and straight lines. Occasionally his arcs and angles give way to less modern lighter pieces adorned with gay flowers and bouquets, but essentially his work is ultra-modern. Luce brought his art to glass. He was not a glass craftsman. Despite this, he has instinctively sensed the limitations and possibilities, and has succeeded in adapting his ideas to glass in effective designs. To those who do not lean his way, some of Luce's curves and cubes are mere crystallized pothooks and nursery blocks but to the "modern" his ideas are approaching a true beauty which will endure.

Jean Sala is one of the few who personally follow the glass from the pre-furnace stage to completion, working decorations into the blown glass while it is hot. Hence his glass is full of originality and cleverness, much of which naturally

FRENCH
Acid etched fruit bowl with undecorated stem and base by Daum Brothers
[PAGE 64]

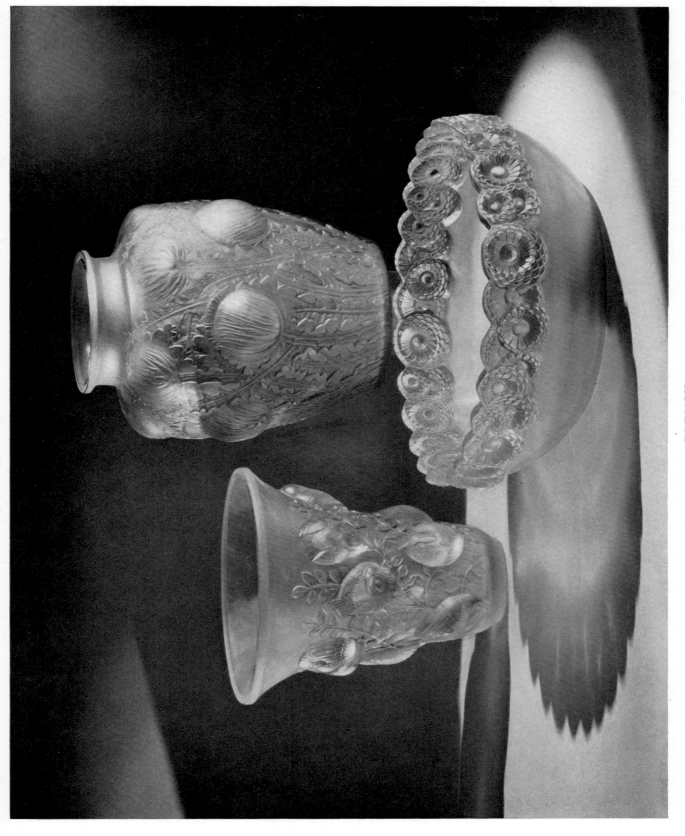

FRENCH

Lalique; molded and engraved pieces in semi-opaque, slightly colored glass

(Courtesy of Ovington's)

[PAGE 65]

is due to the necessary spontaneity entailed by the procedure. The fish motif is one of his favorites.

Other French artists of note in the glass field are M.
Dufrêne, M. Pissaro, H. Farge, and L. Vuitton, exponent of
Negro art. Jean Letard's designs are in the modern manner;
especially interesting are his pieces of simple design on plain
silver bases.

Baccarat. The Compagnie des Cristalleries de Baccarat,
Muerthe et Moselle, France, is one of France's oldest and
finest glass manufactories. Their infinitely varied activities
range from architectural and gross ornamental pieces to
dainty stemware. Baccarat decorative styles include numerous adaptations of prismatic forms and considerable use of a
wider more sweeping type. In much of their ware they
accept the purity of the crystal with little attempt at accen-
tuation, permitting the decorative cuts to follow rather a
design of limited prismatic effect.

The Baccarat artists in their cut crystal have completely
over-stepped many of the traditional limitations imposed by
glass, achieving a heightened vitality which emanates from
subtly calculated sources, especially noticeable in the work
of A. Bullet and G. Chevalier.

Saint Louis. The Verrerie de la Compagnie des Cristalleries de Saint Louis is a branch of the Baccarat firm. One of
their specialties is a layered dark crystal glass. One of
Gallé's pupils, an artist named Nicholas, has engraved much
of this ware. The stamp of the Saint Louis works and the

FRENCH

Left, bottle by Maurice Marinto; center, crystal candlesticks by Jean Luce; right, jar by Henri Navarre; lower, opalescent bowl by René Lalique

influence of Maurice Defrêne are noticeably evident in the glass of the Paris shops.

Verlys was originated in France by the Société Anonyme Holophane, for many years manufacturers of prismatic lighting glassware. Their first production of Verlys, about 1931, was the direct result of a plan for complete utilization of production capacity which was not employed in the manufacture of lighting glassware.

Verlys, which is of both blown and molded types, is essentially a decorative glass. For the most part it is lime base, though lead occasionally is used for technical pur- poses.

Color within the glass—never applied color—is their decorative means of enhancing molded and blown shapes. Heatherish purple vitalizes a thistle motif; an aqueous opalescence lends realism to water subjects, such as lily designs and sea shells, or highly stylized fish and water fowl; while other things of nature are crystallized in amber, topaz, rose and blues, through the magic of the Verlys palette.

Although relatively new in the field of novelty glass, Verlys has achieved a respected position.

Chapter V

HOLLAND AND BELGIUM

HOLLAND

THE seventeenth century saw Dutch glass develop a more indigenous character. Large tulip-shaped glasses appeared, and diamond engravings (scratching) on other shapes eventually displaced the Venetian and German patterns which had been the fashion.

Jacob Sang's excellent glass cutting in the eighteenth century was eclipsed by the new diamond stippled glass, an advance over diamond "scratching." Stippling decoration was accomplished by tapping a diamond pointed instrument over a pattern on the glass; an extremely tedious task bordering on a "penance or a perversion" (the very apt description of W. A. Thorpe). Outstanding exponents of this method, Aert Schouman, D. Wolff, and Frans Greenwood, were able to transfer portraits and other exacting paintings to their glass. Had they been of larger talents and more discerning, they might have left posterity some very indelible Rembrandts.

Following the nineteenth century lull in the glass industry, Holland's revival was headed by H. P. Berlage, an architect, and Gerard Muller, whose artistic creations were at first made in foreign factories. Berlage's water glasses and

DUTCH

Upper left, water set by A. D. Copier, Leerdam; upper right,
center and lower left, specimens of eighteenth century diamond
stippled goblets
(Courtesy of Rijksmuseum, Amsterdam)

Lower right, set by A. D. Copier, Amsterdam

[PAGE 70]

Muller's drinking services met immediate favor with the Dutch.

The Leerdam factory working with the architect, De Bazel, prior to 1923, realigned their ideas and to the present time Leerdam glass has forged ahead. C. de Lorm contributed to Leerdam factory an extremely practical household glass of pleasing lines and designs. Leerdam's much favored flower and fruit designs have come largely from the mind of A. D. Copier. Another brilliant artist, Chris Le Beau, left his imprint on Leerdam wares. Until 1925 he was a linen designer with the Van Dissel firm; on transferring his art and ideas to Leerdam the longer stemmed flowers, twigs, and leaves of linen designs began to appear on the Dutch glass and made an immediately favorable impression. After some years at Leerdam, Le Beau went to the Winterberg Glass Works in Czechoslovakia.

Unica glass, a Copier and Le Beau creation, is an alluring, clouded glass, unique in that the clouded appearance often forms fleeting patterns in the otherwise unclouded glass.

Among modern Dutch glass the work of C. Lanooy, a ceramist, and Jaap Gidding have revived interest in enamelled ware with their artistry at Leerdam; especially effective are Lanooy's fish motifs. C. Agterberg's single black line decoration is striking in its simple dignity; and the bottles and flagons of J. Jongert and F. van Alphen are interesting in conception and design.

DUTCH

Leerdam vases designed by A. D. Copier

[PAGE 72]

DUTCH

An exquisite specimen of Leerdam's Unica glass, designed by Copier and Le Beau

[PAGE 73]

Dutch factories, having mastered practically every known technical glass procedure, now are sagaciously adding the counsel and creative efforts of noted artists. Their present popularity is the deserved increment to this shrewd policy.

BELGIUM

Liège, the seventeenth century glass center of Belgium, produced quantities of glass largely in imitation of the German and Venetian. However, it met little beyond local favor and by 1800 Liège and its glass had lost in the race against the new English flint glass.

Between then and the rise of the industry at Val Saint Lambert, there was only one little glimmering of nice glass, that being at Namur where the Zoude family did some worthwhile work. Here at Namur has been excavated an ancient glass factory possibly of Roman construction.

The Val Saint Lambert factories, founded by the Frenchmen Lelievere and Kemlin in 1825, began their greatest development later when Jules Deprez assumed management. Their exports perhaps exceed those of any other brand. Characterizing the glass are a peculiar ring and a unique limpidity. It appears in a wide range of styles; molded, pressed, and blown, with a full range of decorative schemes. Heavy cut crystal is specialized in at their Walloon Works, also shallow wheel engraving in gossamer designs and lacy traceries. Val Saint Lambert cased glass embodies very real craftsmanship in wheel cutting over the laminated layers of several tints. In this ware colorful jewel effects gleam through the varying depths of the cuts, changing with every light focus. Particularly appealing is the gold and engraved work of K. Graffarth, of Val Saint Lambert.

DUTCH

Duck in plastic glass by Lucienne Block of Leerdam

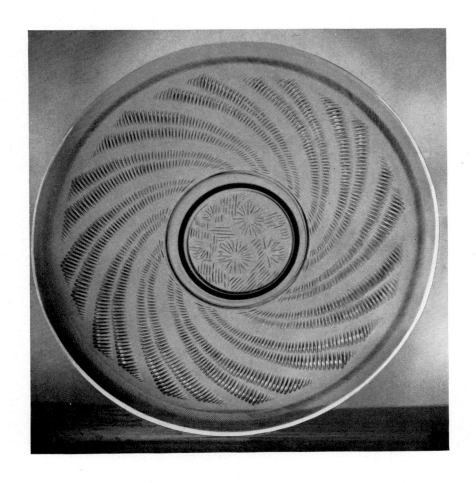

SWEDISH–EDA
Upper, engraved topaz plate by
Gerda Strömberg; lower, bowl
and plate by G. Strandberg

Chapter VI

SWEDEN AND FINLAND

SWEDEN

IN less than two centuries of glass history and a little over three decades in the field of better glass, Sweden has attained an enviable position among the world's fine glassmakers. Swedish glass history is quite fully chronicled in the accounts of the activities of the various factories.

The Eda Glass Works, located in Varmland, was established in 1833. Until rather recently pressed glass was their primary output, but with the management of E. Strömberg they have developed a worthwhile cut glass, characterized by color tones, such as mild topaz, smoke brown, beryl amethyst, and other more or less neutral shades. Although broad facets and gently lobed flutings pervade the Eda designs they are by no means confined to such styles. The highly artistic productions of Gerda Strömberg include graceful shapes imparted to the semi-fused glass free of cutting; and other designs packed with involved geometric cutting, though seldom of prismatic nature.

The Kosta-Reijmyre factory in Småland produces an outstanding cut glass. It is here that the unusual and elegant cut crystal of the artist Elis Bergh is created. Despite its rather recent entry into the realm of cut glass, this company traces its history back to 1741 with the establishment of the old Kosta works at Karlskrona.

The versatile painter, Gunnar Wennerberg, early in the twentieth century designed and decorated some commendable glass pieces patterned after Gallé, but his work ended with a few experiments. Lovely decanters, drinking glasses, and vases are produced by Kosta, almost wholly by hand, except for the limited use of molds for some gross exterior shapes. The artist Ewald Dahlskog has applied his unique broad slashes in characteristic manner to many of Kosta's modern pieces; stylized animals flee from Dahlskog lightning in one design; in another, four seals push a ball amid waving sea grass; and in others he obtains exceptionally pleasing designs by means of shallow wheel engraving.

Orrefors. The period since 1915 records more activity and recognition for Swedish glass than its entire history up to that time. Sweden's rapid rise to prominence, aside from the recent work of Bergh at the Kosta works, can be traced almost directly to the Orrefors factory.

Taking over a tiny industrial glass plant at Orrefors where ink bottles and window glass were made, Johann Ekman of Gothenburg reorganized the plant and personnel, entrusting the direction to two noted artists and decorators, Edvard Hald and Simon Gate. Earliest Orrefors glass consisted chiefly of well shaped household glass, but about the time of the amalgamation with the Stomberg Glass

Fruit bowl by Ewald Dahlskog

Flower vase by Elis Bergh

Bowl by Ewald Dahlskog

[PAGE 79]

Decanter and glasses by Edvard Hald

Bowl by Simon Gate

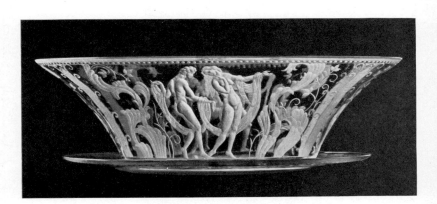

Bowl by Simon Gate

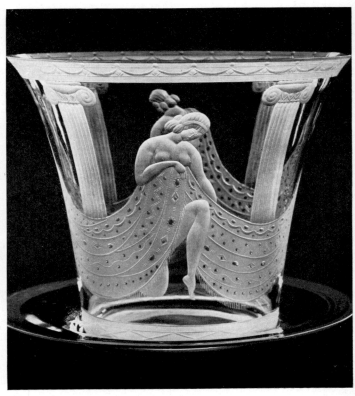

Bowl by Edvard Hald

Works in 1918 there was produced the Orrefors "Graal" glass, an unusual product enshrouded in filmy, cloudy colors and decorative figures. In Graal glass seldom is decoration applied to the cold glass; it is wholly a product of the furnace. Notwithstanding the exacting procedure in making Graal glass and the uncertainty of results, it has continued to be a distinctive feature of the Orrefors production. Later these artists extended their efforts to intaglio engraved glass which with the undecorated colored table glass is now the bulk of Orrefors output.

"To pronounce one or the other (Hald or Gate) as artistically superior is a matter of personal taste. Yet we might perhaps assert that Gate has a clearer perception of the glass in its character of a bubble, whereas Hald's forms reveal a certain curiosity and a quest for the more modern. The decorations of Hald show in a less degree than those of Gate the rich interlacings characteristic of the baroque style, but possess instead a freer imagination which is at the same time more modern and more personal" (from Erik Wettergren's *The Modern Decorative Arts of Sweden*).

Hald and Gate employ methods similar to those used by many sixteenth century Italian intaglio engravers and sculptors of pure rock crystal; especially Gate in his liberal use of the nude human figure, which so ideally complements the intaglio style in the illusion of relief it displays. Hald tends to the more picturesque and fanciful, drawing straight from nature, and depending somewhat upon an imaginative continuance to many of his designs. Gate is more proficient in engraving and cutting along lines of the Renaissance baroque style, especially reminiscent of the Renaissance engravings. Despite all of these influences, and an international training in the case of Hald, the work of these two artists is almost always characteristically Scandinavian. Victor Lindstrand, who came to the Orrefors art staff in 1929, has contributed designs from baroque nudes to highly constrained hand-painted decorations. He ably completes this first triumvirate of Orrefors art.

FINLAND

Karhula glass is a product of the Karhula Company, Karhula, Finland. Established in 1888 by William Ruth, they were soon making worthwhile glass and shortly after the turn of the century their hand-cut lead crystal was competing in world markets—particularly in England. Purity and exceptional clarity—due in part to use of wood as furnace fuel—have always characterized Karhula glass.

Largely dependent upon export outlets, Karhula lines and designs have veered sanely with trade demands. They have, however, retained the indigenous charm of nationality and escaped the label of eclectic art, by shrewdly blending the modern with their own sound basic ideas.

Outstanding in modern Karhula, are the creations of the artists Goran Hongell, Richard Jungell, Y. Rosvall, Mrs. Gunnel Nyman-Gustafsson, Frans Rantanen, and Baron Emil Cedercreutz, the Finnish sculptor: usually their pieces are signed. Rather disposed to flowing curves and animate

Bowl with engraved circus

The Pearl Fisher Vase
by Victor Lindstrond

Caviar bowl by Edvard Hald

Jar by Edvard Hald

SWEDISH–ORREFORS

Engraved crystal bon-bon dish by Richard Jungell

Frosted glass vase, and molded bowl with impressed design, by Mrs. Gunnel Nyman-Gustafsson

(All, Courtesy of Markt and Hammacher)

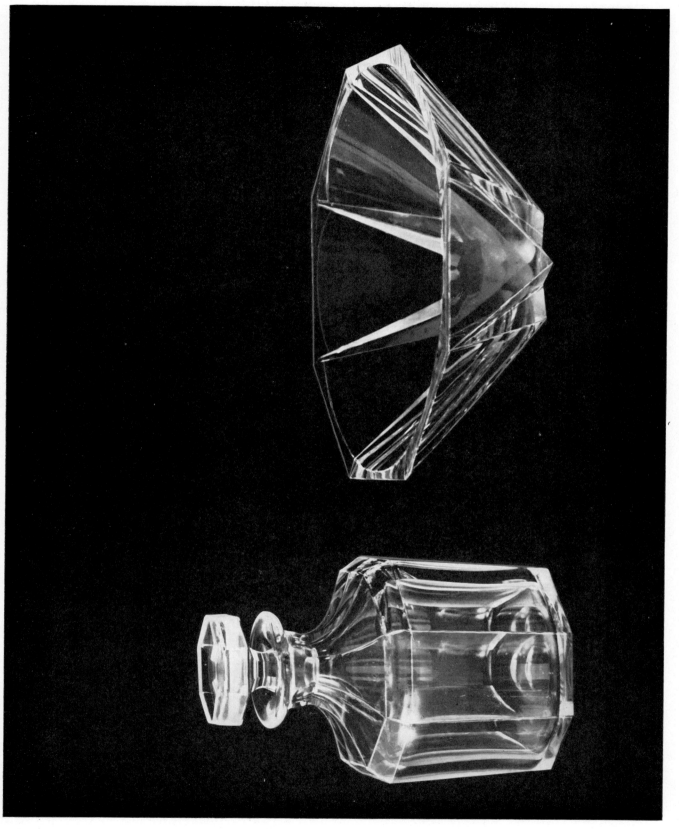

FINNISH

Heavy lead crystal bottle and bowl designed by Richard Jungell for Karhula

(Courtesy of Markt and Hammacher)

[PAGE 85]

subjects, Hongell manages some truly rhythmic composi-
tions based on this particular style. Unspecious aesthetic
balance marks Hongell designs. Harmony of shape and
lines with the purpose of the piece, rather than the solu-
tion of equations of art, endow his glass with appealing
beauty.

Equally attractive but vastly dissimilar is the work of
Jungell. His awareness of the pure transparency of Karhula
glass has led him into designs which serve to heighten that
quality; recurring angles, straight lines and large triangular
areas conspire to glorify the glass *per se*, without overatten-
tion to angularity. Niceties of geometry appearing along
edges, where angular exteriors make the transition to circu-
lar inner surfaces, also tend to show off the glass rather than
the cutter's ability.

To the creative genius of Mrs. Gunnel Nyman-Gustafsson, Karhula is indebted for some splendid designs, distinctive and inspiring in their modernity. In both molded and
engraved designs, she aims at broad effects which are
accomplished with a minimum of lines—suggestive lines
which subtly vary interpretation and heighten aesthetic
values. One of her designs, an irregular shaped shallow bowl
with engraved fish, clearly demonstrates her sure touch and
facility in glass design.

Baron Cedercreutz approaches glass as a sculptor, sub-
ordinating the glass to his ideas and technique; it is another
medium of expression to him, rather than a product to be
decorated or molded by him. Naturally some of his most

FINNISH

Typical and indigenous engraved decorations on Karhula crystal

(*Courtesy of Markt and Hammacher*)

[PAGE 87]

interesting creations are of the solid decorative type—bold lined and grotesque animal designs especially.

Y. Rosvall, the Finnish artist, inclines to the modern in his glass designs. Often he combines with bold lines and slashing strokes some quaint shape which renders the whole most ingenuous; stylized fish, waves and water are among his choice decorative subjects.

At present Mr. Alvar Aalto, the well known Finnish architect, is also working with Karhula.

Interesting unsigned Karhula pieces include vodka sets, lamp bases and utility bowls and vases, appearing in various colors and textures ranging from crystal to highly colored bubble glass, crackle glass and many others of individual charm.

The Osakeyhtiò Riihimaki firm was established in 1910 at Suomi, Finland.

Distinctive features of this glass are its heavy crystal metal, massive shapes, and depth of cutting. When struck, a full-toned ring reveals the high quality of the beautifully clear lead crystal. Although prismatic effects predominate in the extensive wheel cutting, many novel naturalistic lines and designs occur throughout the ware; and the decorative schemes are remarkably compatible with the proportions of the pieces. Recent American demand for Finnish glass, has perhaps led Riihimaki designers somewhat away from their older glyptic styles which formerly found especial favor in England.

FINNISH

Engraved vase by Frans Rantanen and shallow bowl in heavy crystal by Mrs. Gunnel Nyman-Gustafsson, both Karhula

(Courtesy of Markt and Hammacher)

[PAGE 89]

FINNISH

Decanter and stemware in Karhula crystal

(Courtesy of Markt and Hammacher)

[PAGE 90]

FINNISH
Cut crystal by Riihimaki
(Courtesy of J. H. Venon)
[PAGE 91]

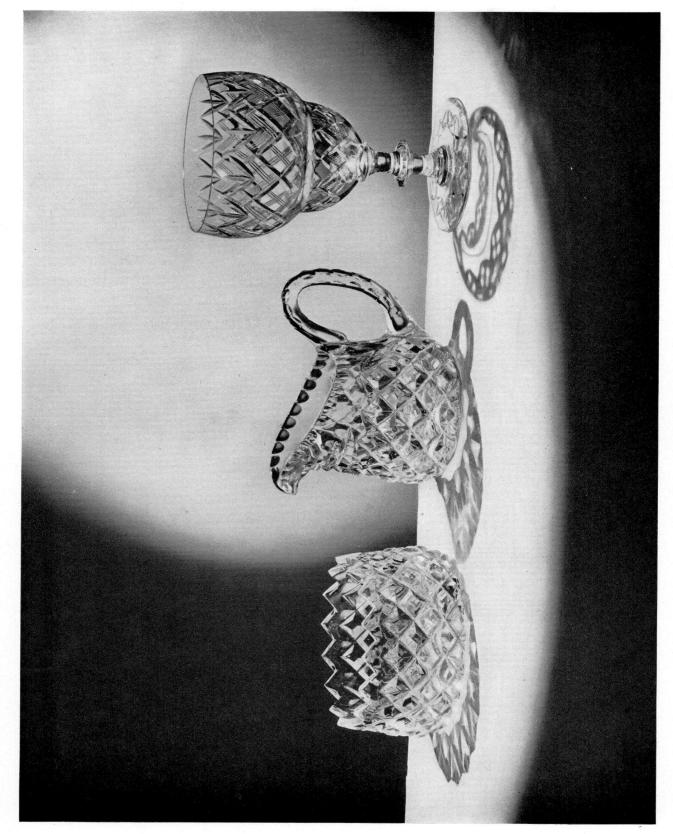

FINNISH
Heavy cut crystal by Riihimaki
(Courtesy of J. H. Venon)

[PAGE 92]

Chapter VII

ENGLAND

ALTHOUGH dim and meager, there is evidence that the Romans had engaged in glassmaking in England before their exodus in 407 A.D. It is not unlikely that the old works unearthed at Warrington and Wilderspool were direct outgrowths of some of the ancient Roman factories; up to the Renaissance, however, there was little other glass activity in England. The sixteenth century tankard in the British Museum dated 1586 is one of the earliest pieces of exact dating, though historical records disclose the presence of many glassworkers earlier. Drawings and descriptions of their glass show it to have been fashioned largely after Venetian, which was a less ornate glass in those days.

The Italian glass imported in large quantities continued to compete with its English imitations until the Bohemian cut crystal entered the Island during the seventeenth century. Veering the fashion to heavy cut crystal, this ware blazed a golden path for the glistening English "flint glass."

It was in 1675 that George Ravenscroft, with the assistance of the Italian De Costa, produced "flint glass" by the addition of lead oxide to ordinary glass ingredients. Lead glass has extremely high dispersive powers, and additional luster though it is heavier and less tough than lime glass; but for the subsequent English style of cutting it was ideal.

Early in the eighteenth century glass cutting and engraving made long strides in England due, in part, to the richer and more inviting surface of the new flint glass, and, to some extent, to the influence and patterns of the Bohemian cutting. By 1750 English and Irish flint had largely displaced Bohemian glass in European markets. From the simple motifs like rose branches, butterflies, moths, mottoes, et cetera, the cutting and engraving advanced by 1800 to the prismatic cuts; convex, raised diamond patterns, and other intricate operations. Quantities of the finest English and Irish flint glass of this time were coming from Stourbridge, Dublin, Bristol, Cork, Belfast, and Waterford, much of which now bears the Waterford label, though this plant opened in 1783, some years after flint glass had actually reached its zenith. Bristol was also noted for its enamelled and colored ware; royal blue, deep cherry red, and beautiful opaque enamelled glass. As a rule it was less expensive than cut glass; therefore it graced many middle class tables. At Nailsea, glass of the Bristol type appeared. It favored colors and Venetian styles in both the utility ware and novelty glass.

When steam took over the task of whirling the cutting discs and grinding wheels, more and deeper cutting naturally followed, adding to brilliancy and prismatic effects.

Soon, however, the cutting became so bizarre as to border on the grotesque, and reaction set in, hastened by Ruskin's caustic writings on the subject.

Whitefriars. This excessive cutting soon gave way to more subdued designs in which the cutting was more in keeping with the form and purpose of the piece. Noteworthy along this line is the recent work of Barnaby Powell, of the Whitefriars, Ltd., who lets the cutting wheel take a more natural path across the surface of the glass, thus producing more light and airy designs, and less of the purely geometric. The Whitefriars glassworks was founded in London in 1680 and until 1845 made flint glass almost exclusively. The unusual brilliance of their glass is largely the result of close adherence to basic laws of optics and mathematics in guiding their cutting wheels. Stained glass for windows is fully as important in their work as the making of table and decorative glass.

The Stevens & Williams firm, established in 1776 under the name of Honeybourne, is among the leading English glassmakers. Their cameo glass was brought to perfection by John Northwood, who first reproduced the Portland Vase in glass (Wedgwood reproduced it in pottery). Among Stevens & Williams' various other methods of decoration are: intaglio, used principally on vases, bowls, et cetera; gilding, and etching often used on stoppered utensils, also on imitation rock crystal. Much of their glass is characterized by an appearance of sturdiness in design and decoration, although infinite delicacy abound in other pieces. Recently Mr. Keith Murray, a London architect, has collaborated on some fresh designs for Stevens & Williams, in which flat cutting has largely displaced the "flashy cutting." Some of this new glass is extremely thin, with delicate flat cutting; other heavier pieces depend on simplicity of facets or restrained engraved designs. Of colored ware produced by Stevens & Williams, that of the delightful buttercup yellow tint is especially noteworthy.

Thomas Webb & Sons was established in 1837; the present owners are Webb's Crystal Glass Co., Ltd. of London, and The Edinburgh & Leith Flint Glass Works of Edinburgh. This firm has long made excellent table glass; finely wrought bits of crystal executed by hand, goblets, decanters, bottles, and flat pieces; candlesticks which follow old "Anglo-Venetian" designs, flower holders, et cetera, in limitless variety, all emphasizing utility with beauty. "Thomas Webb cut glass designs, far from multiplying the points of illumination, tend rather to accentuate the form itself." Webb glass is truly hand made. They depend entirely on calipers, paddles, and other hand tools to produce the gross shapes of their pieces, even shunning the use of molds which are openly accepted by many manufacturers as legitimate tools of hand workmanship. Webb's glass is famed for its exquisite polish and crystal purity and the avoidance of the more stereotyped flashy cuttings.

Many replicas of old patterns are faithfully reproduced in

ENGLISH
Modern design decanter and glass by Stevens and Williams
[PAGE 97]

ENGLISH

Webb-Corbett; goblets and sherbets in hand cut and engraved heavy lead crystal.
Stem and foot of each are cut and engraved. Upper center is a modern "John
Greene" funnel shape with cut flutings continuing from stem up the bowl

(Courtesy of Tiffany and Company)

ENGLISH

Upper left, replicas of Victorian decanters by Thomas Webb and Sons; upper right, decanters and glasses by Whitefriars; center, decanter, pitcher and glasses by Stevens and Williams; lower, engraved decanter and stemware by Webb and Corbett

[PAGE 99]

goblets and a variety of other pieces by the Edinburgh & Leith Glass Company.

Thomas Webb and Corbett, Ltd., was founded in 1897 by the brothers Thomas and Herbert Webb, sons of the nineteenth century glassmaker, Thomas Wilkes Webb. The firm commenced business in Brewery Street, Wordsley, near Stourbridge, England, specializing in cut and engraved lead crystal. By 1900 they had built up a considerable home and export business, especially with their polished rock crystal engraving, which found a ready market in the United States.

At Coalbournhill, their site since 1913, some 550 glassworkers fulfill the very exacting conceptions of Webb-Corbett artists and designers, to produce a glass of resplendent beauty, universally recognized as one of the finest glasses in the world.

Specializing in decorated heavy lead crystal, they have noticeably veered away from the older prismatic cutting to lighter, airy designs which ideally complement especially their thinner metal stemware. Dainty buds, flowing tendrils, stems and tiny leaves are recurring motifs in many of Webb-Corbett's most appealing designs. Highly polished designs of this type on pure lead crystal impart amazing brilliance to the glass—something in the nature of a sparkling liquidity.

Although Webb-Corbett have been among the leaders of English glassmakers to depart from so much of the heavy

ENGLISH
Hand cut engraved lead crystal by Walsh Walsh

[PAGE 101]

Flecked and marbled "monart bowl" by John Moncrieff (Scotland)

Massive cut center bowl by Thomas Webb and Sons

Heavy engraved bowl by T. Webb and Corbett

prismatic cutting, they make glass for that demand and do considerable in the way of reproductions; certainly their Waterford reproductions gloriously restore and endear that noble old type. Summing up Webb-Corbett glass, it is little less than an artistic triumph. From a charming austerity in one design they turn to one of imposing simplicity: in other designs they boldly aim at the grandiose, shrewdly avoiding any semblance of ponderous elegance through subtle mollifying lines in shape or decoration.

Webb-Corbett glass truly reveals a remarkable skill in handling the materials of this art.

John Walsh Walsh, Ltd. (Soho and Vesta Glassworks), of Birmingham, England, has been in business since 1801, continuing under the direction of the members of John Walsh Walsh's family without a break since its foundation.

Walsh Walsh crystal glassware is entirely a handmade product, which interprets the spirit of the age, or reproduces "period" glass with utmost accuracy. Skillful cutting on well shaped, crystal clear glass may be considered a fair, unqualified definition of Walsh Walsh glass. Although prismatic form and that type cutting has been rather completely exploited, this firm is remarkably successful in its continuance. Intangibly, their highly refractive ware reflects utter confidence in their ability to outdo others using the same tools and materials.

Essentially their decorations are deep cut on rather thick metal, but they belie any such characterization in their airy little animal figures of blown opaque glass; and their uncommonly beautiful colored glass of lighter metals.

John Moncrieff, Ltd., Perth, Scotland. In 1924 this old firm of industrial glassmakers entered the decorative field with their "Monart glass," a distinctive colored product. In it the color has been incorporated into the body of the handmade glass, to attain amazing effects; flecks, marbling, streaked glass—random or controlled in design—and innumerable other striking color patterns. As yet the production is largely confined to lamps, flower bowls, jars, and ornamental pieces.

Chapter VIII

AMERICA

GLASSMAKING in America prior to the seventeenth century amounted to little more than a few sporadic attempts, each of which ended in failure because of the lack of trained and interested workmen. Glass utensils were used in the seventeenth century, but their use was confined largely to the tables of wealthy colonists who imported a few pieces from London.

The glassworks established at Jamestown, Virginia, in 1609 by some Dutch and Polish glassblowers should probably be honored as the first American glass works, though it was short lived. Following this was the polyglot attempt in 1621, when imported Venetian workmen from London made Italian beads for American trade with the Indians. After the failure of the bead venture the year 1641 saw the next enterprise, that of O. Holmes and L. Southwick at Salem, Massachusetts, where some crude pieces, later found in that vicinity, were supposed to have originated.

In 1645 Glassmakers Street in New Amsterdam started operations which continued to the eve of the Revolution. The old Dutch glassworkers, Smedes, Dirkson, the Jansens, and the Melyns, naturally patterned their work almost wholly after Holland glass.

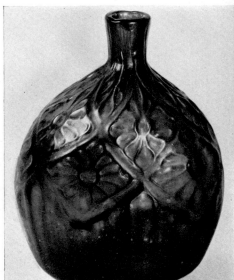

AMERICAN

Upper left, Stiegel toilet water bottle of purple glass blown in mold, 1763–1764;
right, Wistarberg green bottle, mid eighteenth century
(Both, Courtesy of Metropolitan Museum of Art)

Center, vase with thistle design by Verlys of America; lower, set of ornamental
flower bowls in crystal by Steuben
(Verlys, Courtesy of Ovington's)

Before 1825 the ideas and designs of foreign workers so permeated American glass that, instead of having an individuality of its own, it embodied a welter of European decorative ideas and lines—some good and others not.

Wistarberg glass came from the furnace of Caspar and Richard Wistar which operated from 1738 to 1780, though little table glass was blown until 1752. This rugged, serviceable Wistarberg flint glass of pre-Revolutionary days quite faithfully expressed the spirit of those pioneers whose serious efforts for existence kept them too occupied to produce or fully appreciate much other than essentials. Although restraint ruled their inherent aesthetic sense, it was fully revealed in the simple decorations they did employ. Perhaps the most characteristic features of Wistarberg glass were: the unusual over-layers of glass partially covering some pieces; the spiral glass cord encircling bottle necks, mugs, and pitchers; the decorative designs of delicately drawn out waves and lily pads; and the extensive use of colored glass, among which the turquoise, amber, and green were exceptionally lovely.

Following Wistarberg came Stiegel glass, also a truly American product, but of more European conception and execution than the Wistarberg. This glass had its beginnings in 1765 at Mannheim, Pennsylvania, where H. W. Stiegel and his assemblage of English, Bavarian, and Venetian craftsmen produced an exquisite lead flint glass, to which they added designs of more formal and sophisticated nature than had previously appeared on American glass. In 1769

Stiegel established a larger works following the failure of his first venture. Despite the persistent foreign influence in Stiegel glass it developed an unmistakably American character. Striking examples were the sturdy mold pattern pieces bearing the Bristol imprint, and the very marked German and Swiss stamp of the enamelled and etched glass.

Following the invention of the glasspressing machine and process in 1827 at Sandwich, Massachusetts, the United States was flooded with the new pressed glass and its machine impressions. Historical objects, emblems and national heroes flashed from pitchers, mugs, whisky flasks and the quaint old cup plates. By the middle of the nineteenth century pressed glass was produced in most of the larger glass works, many of them abandoning wholly the blowing process while others compromised between blowing and pressing. Moderation gradually crept into the decorations and designs to soften somewhat crass excesses, and eventually pressed glass developed a not too objectionable mien. Linked with exceptional durability was the infinite range of selection in shapes, colors, designs, and pieces.

Between 1880 and 1890, concurrent with much of William Morris's revolutionizing work in English decorative arts, there appeared in America the first run of commercial cut glass. This immediately followed the discovery of a fine sand almost free of iron oxide. Despite the overworked prismatic and star cuts, the crystalline purity of the metal was tremendously appealing. It soon commanded world recognition and respect. Great quantities originated at the Libbey firm in Toledo, Ohio. Tiffany favrile glass of the gay, swirling and mystical colors also appeared about this time. The increasing demand, however, resulted in quantity production by means of machine stamping on pressed figure blanks, which were later cut over by hand. As this machine work, at best, did not compare with hand cutting, the popularity of American cut glass soon waned. Very likely even a perfect machine reproduction of the hand work would have met a similar fate; not infrequently its very abundance, partially obscures commonplace beauty. Nevertheless hand cut glass was continued and improved by a few American manufacturers, whose discreet intaglio engraving and copper wheel cutting enhanced their crystal and colored wares.

Bryce glass is made by the Bryce Brothers Company of Mount Pleasant, Pennsylvania, glassmakers for over ninety years. Largely confined to blown stemware, they have formulated a partial lead content glass which imparts remarkable clarity to the glass. When struck, it gives off the characteristic lead glass tone. Ranging from the older, heavy cut Waterford styles, down to ultramodern shapes and decorations, Bryce glass fulfills most demands of good taste. Restraint in cutting, judicious use of color, and a lustrous finish, achieved through mechanical and hand polishing, place this glass in competition with many wares of higher lead content.

The Cambridge Glass Company was established at Cambridge, Ohio, in 1901. Their production consists of pressed

AMERICAN
An unusual design by Cambridge
[PAGE 110]

AMERICAN

Dinnerware in etched glass by Cambridge

[PAGE 113]

and blown glass of either lime or lead base. Etching, coloring, cutting, gold decoration, and enamelling comprise the bulk of their decorations.

In their colors, Cambridge royal blue is derived from zaffer, forest green from chrome oxide, amber from sulphur, and selenium produces their beautiful peach-blo. Cambridge glass is perhaps most characterized by its unusual colors, intricate and lacy acid etchings, remarkable transparency even in the pressed wares, and the precise and pleasing designs of their cut crystal.

In pressed ware, which is a considerable portion of their production, they heed aesthetic satisfaction by adapting utilitarian grace to the lines and shapes of the pieces. The Cambridge designers sense that duplication of a beautiful shape or design can escape banality, when the original is truly beautiful and the reproduction authentic.

The Fostoria Glass Company, at Moundsville, West Virginia, was moved shortly after its establishment at Fostoria, Ohio, in 1887. West Virginia natural gas, so important in glass polishing, and as a source of fuel at that time, was largely responsible for the re-location.

Fostoria glass is made with both lead and lime base, pressed glass employing lime and the blown, lead. All Fostoria glass is handmade, even their pressed ware is produced in hand-operated presses. The origination of glass dinnerware is claimed by Fostoria, also the distinction of being the first American works to make colored ware popular. Their register of colors runs from dainty rose, azure, wisteria, through the brighter greens, topaz, and ambers to an opaque ebony.

Variety is quite unlimited in Fostoria glass: massive cut rock crystal centerpieces, lovely pressed candlesticks, fragile blown figurines, and other bits of real craftsmanship are produced along with their lustrous colored dinnerware and brilliant stemware.

Particularly noteworthy are Fostoria's splendid plate etchings (the term plate here refers to the steel engraving plate employed in the process), made by a delicate process of acid engraving in which intricate designs are transferred to glass. Needle etching, a less intricate method, is also an effective decorative process used by Fostoria.

Other Fostoria glass is beautified by wheel cutting, especially the rock crystal pieces; still others are decorated with applied colors for effects of iridescence, and other color attributes. Lastly should be mentioned the less common but striking applied metallic decorations.

The polish, a noticeable and distinguishing feature of Fostoria glass, is accomplished by utmost care and working of the glass over a natural gas flame (this is their only use for natural gas now) which adds luster and brilliancy never equalled in machine polished products.

The grace and logic of design of Fostoria heavier pressed pieces, namely, cups, saucers, plates, bowls, and such pieces, have noticeably reduced the old and prevalent feeling against pressed glass—a prejudice partly based on the

AMERICAN
Double candlesticks by Fostoria
(Courtesy of Ovington's)
[PAGE 114]

AMERICAN
Water set by Fostoria
(Courtesy of Ovington's)
[PAGE 115]

assumption that scarcity enters into aesthetic appraisal and appeal.

T. G. Hawkes and Company, established in 1880 at Corning, New York, trace their glass heritage back through some of the world's finest cut glass to the "Old Singing Waterford," an earlier product of Hawkes, which name is also associated with the first fine Waterford flint glass in 1783. Unquestionably Hawkes led the Americans in cut glass prestige at the close of the nineteenth century, as attested by Hawkes' capture of the grand prize at the 1889 Paris Exposition. At present, although Hawkes largely confine their activities to decorating, their specifications dictate the clarity of the crystal they use.

All this glass tradition is reflected in Hawkes' modern cut crystal and the amazingly transparent colored glass they use; also true craftsmanship is evident in their sumptuous pieces decorated with applied precious metals and their occasional fine work in enamelling. Amidst all this gorgeous glass, however, Hawkes' outstanding work is their rock crystal cutting, ranging from heavier cut old Waterford reproductions to the more modern types, cut in lighter and more figurative designs. Hawkes' faithful reproductions of old Waterford are surpassed only by their modern glass in its greater deference to that crowning attribute of "rock crystal"—its inherent transparency. Geometrical designs, so often running into the almost banal star pattern of the late nineteenth century cut glass, have given place to more animated irregular lines of leaves, flowers, vines, et cetera, in Hawkes' modern cut crystal. And their reproductions for the most part are taken from specimens of old glass which were not the playground for abstract meandering of the cutting wheel, but rather of pleasing lines of full prismatic effect. Ruskin's castigation of cut glass and its users might have been less acrid had the cutting on Victorian goblets been as restrained as on these Hawkes' reproductions.

The artistic genius of Samuel Hawkes is chiefly responsible for the designs and decorative ideas of Hawkes' glass. In all their glass one senses this guiding mind so open to innovation though tempered with sane conservatism.

The A. H. Heisey Company was established in 1893 at Newark, Ohio. Lead blown and pressed glass constitute the major part of their output. The former, which they term a "lead blown potash glass," is a high quality ware not unlike much of the French and Belgian blown ware in purity, ring, and metal. Certain Heisey secrets linked with unusual refinements of raw materials and polishing processes impart a challenging beauty to their table glass.

Heisey colors practically embrace the full range of the requirements of good taste; from uncolored crystal to the flushed darker hues, they have achieved exceptional brilliance. For instance their mystical plum (bluish red) hue with its flashy overtone of amethyst under artificial light; the brilliant emerald; and the very individual Heisey tangerine shade. Besides these, their rose, amber, blue, and a

AMERICAN
Cut crystal vase by Hawkes; urn type vase in crystal by Pairpoint
(Courtesy of Ovington's)
[PAGE 118]

AMERICAN
Salad bowl in "Saturn optic" by A. H. Heisey and Company
[PAGE 119]

AMERICAN

Evolution of cut crystal goblet by T. G. Hawkes and Company

[PAGE 120]

AMERICAN

Double candlesticks and flower bowl in cut crystal by Heisey

[PAGE 121]

sandy golden shade are rare examples of crystalline beauty; all quite distinctive and individual, even the lovely rose which has been so widely copied. Together with crystal cutting, Heisey decorations include both single and double etchings and an "all over" etching process. They rarely do enamelling.

The Libbey Glass Manufacturing Company of Toledo, Ohio, is the outgrowth of the old New England Glass Company of South Boston, established in 1818 and acquired by William L. Libbey in 1855. In 1888 when natural gas became so plentiful in Ohio, the company moved to Toledo.

Early in this century the Libbey interests veered almost exclusively to machine production glass, which has continued with only occasional forays into the realm of fine glass. Between 1932 and 1934, under the art guidance of A. Douglas Nash, their experiments and activities in this field were rather spirited, but with subsequent changes in company policies their fine table glass production has been largely discontinued.

The Pairpoint Corporation of New Bedford, Massachusetts, was established in 1865. Inasmuch as they make no pressed glass, Pairpoint is almost exclusively a lead base product. All blanks are made by free hand blowing or blowing into plain molds; those of heavy metal are ordinarily decorated by deep cutting, while the lighter blanks are dec-

AMERICAN

Punch bowl with cover and custard set by Heisey

[PAGE 123]

AMERICAN
Engraved crystal by Heisey
(Courtesy of Ovington's)
[PAGE 124]

AMERICAN
Candelabra bobache and "D" prisms by Heisey
[PAGE 125]

AMERICAN

Two-light candelabra in cut crystal with prisms, by Heisey

[PAGE 126]

AMERICAN

Salad bowl, goblet and saucer champagne by Heisey

[PAGE 127]

orated by stone engraving of the rock crystal type cutting. In Pairpoint's deep cut heavy crystal the designs are quite freed of the excessive prismatic precision of the glistening nineties. The noble old pin wheels, stars, and fans have given way to more natural lines; lines which harmonize with shapes and enhance transparency rather than create over-dazzling effects.

Glyptic facets and highly polished nodules "en cabo-chon" under modern artificial lights are considerably more ostentatious than they were under the dimmer, yellow lights of the nineties. Happily, Pairpoint designers maintain a sat-isfying balance between brilliance and aesthetic cutting. Especially attractive among Pairpoint cut decorations is the gray cut design; this effect is achieved by smoothing the cuts with a stone instead of polishing to transparency.

Cobalt blue and light ruby are perhaps the most char-acteristic colors of Pairpoint glass. Little or no enamelling is done at present.

The Steuben Division of Corning Glass Works, Corning, New York, was established in 1903 by Frederick Carder. In 1918 the Corning Glass Works acquired controlling interest of Steuben.

Steuben is almost entirely hand-made, blown glass of lead base. No painted or enamelled decorations are employed and within the last few years even colored glass has been largely discontinued as a stock product, although formerly this was one of the glories of Steuben.

Like other glassmakers, Steuben have constantly striven to produce a perfectly transparent crystal—a glass inherently beautiful in its clarity—which would invite and challenge artists as a superior medium of expression.

Nothing better attests the fulfillment of these aims than modern Steuben crystal itself. Under the direction of Arthur A. Houghton, Jr., John M. Gates and Sidney B. Waugh, Steuben designs not only enhance the pure transparency of the glass, but also noticeably extend the limits of art in its applications to glass.

Architecturally trained, Mr. Gates has brought majestic, flowing lines to his glass designs as well as an amazing sense of proportion between elements of decoration and the shape of the piece. His heavy cut crystal vase, designed for the Paris International Exposition of 1937, is a superb tribute to his style and an object of genuine beauty; seldom does an artist invest matter with such an abundance of grace as Mr. Gates has achieved in this magnificent creation. Another masterpiece to which he lent his talents is the massive crystal bowl in the permanent collection of Contemporary American glass in the Metropolitan Museum of Art.

The designs of Mr. Waugh, the young American sculptor, are characterized by engraved decorations of his own unique conception. Drawing upon mythology, legend, allegory, and constantly upon that supreme motif of the sculptor—the human body—his varied and animated designs constitute a new trend in American glass. Exotic beings arrested in capricious bits of fantasy; fabulous episodes from mythology; or symbolic designs such as his Mariner's bowl are favorites of Mr. Waugh.

In his work, although the glass is noticeably a background for the cut decoration, there is in every piece a satisfying unity which fully harmonizes the nature of the engraving with the design as a whole. Aesthetic deference of the ornament to the ornamented is evident in all the work of Mr. Waugh.

Some day—not too remote—when Steuben's disappearing colored glass will be at a premium, the name of Frederick Carder will also stand out among Steuben artists for his part in perfecting that glass. Since 1933 the directing genius of Arthur A. Houghton, Jr., has been associated with the creative zeal of Mr. Gates and Mr. Waugh. Mr. Houghton, a vice-president of Corning Glass, has brought both enthusiasm and a fine appreciation of true hand-craftsmanship to the task of supervising the select group of Steuben artisans.

Steuben crystal is a vital source of inspiration to these three men: Houghton, Gates and Waugh. Through an active interchange of ideas between themselves and other artists, and with uncanny awareness of the beauty of pure crystal, they have heightened that beauty by means of truly aesthetic designs—designs of utter charm and originality which are subtly more appealing for their gracious subservience to the crystal they enhance.

Throughout Steuben designs their engraving, cutting and shaping are noticeably executed by craftsmen who are interested in capturing the exact spirit of the designer; they

AMERICAN

Engraved crystal stemware set by Steuben

[PAGE 131]

AMERICAN

Irregular shaped crystal vase, formed by twirling the molten glass on end of blow pipe, which is then trimmed and footed. Produced by Steuben

[PAGE 132]

AMERICAN

Steuben; massive crystal gazelle bowl, resting on base of solid crystal, designed by Sidney Waugh

[PAGE 133]

AMERICAN

The Mariner's bowl designed by Sidney Waugh for Steuben; a copper wheel-engraved design of a celebrated mariner's compass, encircled by appropriate ornamental and symbolic figures—all on pure crystal

[PAGE 134]

AMERICAN

Stemware set engraved crystal by Steuben

[PAGE 135]

AMERICAN

The Metropolitan Museum of Art, in its permanent collection of contemporary American glass, has the only specimen of this heavy massive bowl, fashioned of clear crystal by the Steuben Division of The Corning Glass Works. No other copy of the bowl was made

(Courtesy of Metropolitan Museum of Art)

[PAGE 136]

inject no jarring interpolations of techinque to unbalance the composition. This sympathetic understanding between designer and cutter frees Steuben of those unbearable banalities which frequently creep in where such cooperation is missing.

Aside from reproductions of earlier types, the Steuben cutting wheels seldom find their paths over the older and arid prismatic routes. Cooperating with designers, the cutters follow, rather, the modern conception of glass cutting, in which cutting is secondary to aesthetic congruity. A bit unmodern, these craftsmen have a wholesome horror of the facile short-cuts of quantity production.

Verlys of America is a product of the Verlys division of the Holophane Glass Company, Newark, Ohio, which in turn is associated with the Société Anonyme Holophane of Les Andelys, France, parent company of Verlys of France.

Inasmuch as Verlys of America, in general, use the designs and molds of their French company, the American product differs only slightly from the French Verlys, which is described under French glass. Verlys of America produces molded glass only, whereas the French company makes considerable blown ware. The American Verlys is producing some interesting applied color designs (the French company does none of this). In this process, a frit composed of finely ground glass and an oil color is applied to the undecorated cold glass. When refired at low temperature this colored frit fuses into the glass while the oil oxidizes, leaving the desired color as part of the original glass. Verlys of America produce their appealing new color "dusty rose" by this process.

With the exceptions of American Verlys blue and amber, which are somewhat deeper than the French Verlys, colors in Verlys glass are all derived from the French company's formulas. Hence the discussion of colors in connection with Verlys of France also applies to Verlys of America.

All American Verlys is hand signed. The name Verlys is scratched in with diamond pencil; the French ware ordinarily carries only a mold impressed signature.

MEXICO

Mexican glassmaking was perhaps brought to Mexico from Spain, although the present glass is less sophisticated than the earlier Spanish-Mexican glass.

Mexican glass, whether made in Guadalajara, Mexico City, or Jalisco or some other place is characteristically the same; variations appear in craftsmanship and materials, but essentially Mexican glass is of light weight, bubbly texture and for the most part in the cooler blues, greens, ambers, and reds with just occasional production in other hues. Shapes are generous and utilitarian and ordinarily marked by spiral swirls and whorls. Most of it is hand blown, with not too much attention to symmetry or academic art principles. Nevertheless it has a peculiar charm which ideally complements a table set with some of the coarser stone and earthenwares on rough or homespun fabrics.

AMERICAN

Upper left, engraved crystal vase by Pairpoint; upper right, bowl; center, bowl by
Verlys of America; lower, bowls and glass by Fostoria

Mexican glass is largely the product of the craftsman who continues the traditional shapes and colors, unmolested by experimenting artists and innovators. Perhaps the most typical and oft-recurring design is the Virgin of Guadalupe bottle, on which the patron saint is impressed in flowing garments.

AMERICAN

Novelty glass in various colors by Verlys of America

(Courtesy of Ovington's)

[PAGE 141]

AMERICAN

The Europa bowl depicts an ancient myth—the carrying away of Europa to Crete by the god Zeus disguised as a bull. Designed by Sidney Waugh for Steuben

[PAGE 142]

INDEX